Get Active!

Louise Spilsbury

Crabtree Publishing Company

www.crabtreebooks.com

Author: Louise Spilsbury
Editor: Crystal Sikkens
Project coordinator: Kathy Middleton
Production coordinator: Ken Wright
Prepress technician: Margaret Amy Salter
Series consultant: Gill Matthews

Every effort has been made to trace copyright holders and to obtain their permission for use of copyright material. The authors and publishers would be pleased to rectify any error or omission in future editions. All the Internet addresses given in this book were correct at the time of going to press. The author and publishers regret any inconvenience caused if addresses have changed or sites have ceased to exist, but can accept no responsibility for any such changes.

Picture credits:
Fotolia: Michael Chamberlin 19
Shutterstock: (Cover), Photocreo MichalBednarek 5,
    Linda Bucklin 7, Jacek Chabraszewski 10, 20,
    Vince Clements 14, Stephen Coburn16–17,
    Sonya Etchison 21, Mandy Godbehear 8, 18,
    Gregory Kendall 17, John Lumb 6,
    Monkey Business Images 4–5, Paulaphoto 12–13,
    Julián Rovagnati 15, Suzanne Tucker 13
Illustration: Geoff Ward 11

Library and Archives Canada Cataloguing in Publication

Spilsbury, Louise
    Get active! / Louise Spilsbury.

(Crabtree connections)
Includes index.
ISBN 978-0-7787-9941-2 (bound).--ISBN 978-0-7787-9963-4 (pbk.)

    1. Exercise--Juvenile literature. 2. Exercise--Health aspects--
Juvenile literature. I. Title. II. Series: Crabtree connections

RA781.S65 2010   j613.7'1   C2010-901522-3

Library of Congress Cataloging-in-Publication Data

Spilsbury, Louise.
    Get active! / Louise Spilsbury.
        p. cm. -- (Crabtree connections)
    Includes index.
    ISBN 978-0-7787-9963-4 (pbk. : alk. paper) -- ISBN 978-0-7787-9941-2
(reinforced library binding : alk. paper)
    1. Exercise for children--Juvenile literature. 2. Physical fitness--
Juvenile literature. I. Title. II. Series.

RJ133.S66 2011
613.7'042--dc22

                                    2010008063

Crabtree Publishing Company

Printed in the U.S.A./062010/WO20100815

Published in Canada
Crabtree Publishing
616 Welland Ave.
St. Catharines, Ontario
L2M 5V6

Published in the United States
Crabtree Publishing
PMB 59051
350 Fifth Avenue, 59th Floor
New York, New York 10118

Contents

Why You Should Get Active

If you leave your bike in the garage for too long it will go rusty and the tires will go flat. Your body is a bit like that, too. You need to use it often to keep it working properly. If you sit around all day you will become unfit.

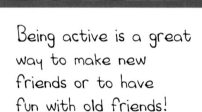

Being active is a great way to make new friends or to have fun with old friends!

There are a lot of reasons to get active:
- It makes you feel good
- It makes you healthy and strong
- It gives you **energy**
- It keeps you from becoming overweight

What's it all about?

This book will show you how being active helps your body. We will suggest different kinds of exercise to try. If you follow the tips in this book and get active, you will feel good, look good, and be healthy.

Being active helps you sleep better. This is important because your body needs rest at night to help you keep going in the day.

Building Muscles and Bones

When you are active your **muscles** and **bones** get bigger and stronger.

On the move

Bones are hard and strong. They form the **skeleton** that holds your body up. Bones are attached to muscles. Muscles are stretchy. They pull on the bones to make them move. When the bones move, your body moves!

Gymnasts are flexible. Being active will help to keep your body **limber** so you can bend and twist.

Work that body

Your bones grow when you are young. This is how you get taller. You need strong bones to support your growing body. Having strong muscles is also important. Strong muscles are less likely to get injured and can work for longer periods of time.

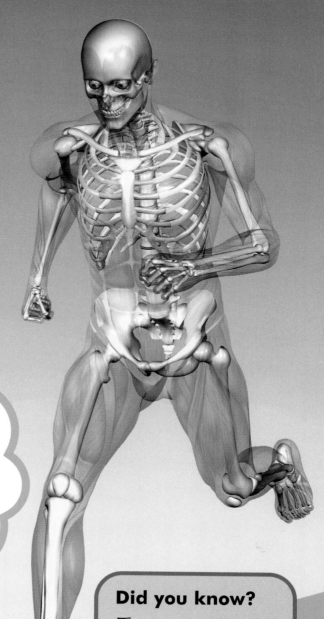

Without the bones and muscles inside your body, you would be as wobbly as jelly and you would not be able to move!

Did you know?
There are 27 bones in one human hand and 14 in the face!

Exercise is Good for Your Heart

Put your hand on your chest.
Can you feel your **heart** beating?
Your heart is a muscle that moves.
Like any other muscle, the heart needs
to be active to stay strong and healthy.

Healthy hearts

You need a healthy heart because it has
a vital job to do. The heart pumps **blood**
around your body. Blood carries food and
oxygen to the rest of the body. The body
uses food and oxygen to make energy.
Energy allows the body to keep working
and to build and repair itself.

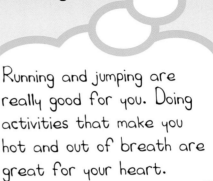

Running and jumping are
really good for you. Doing
activities that make you
hot and out of breath are
great for your heart.

Make your heart race

The best exercises for the heart are those that make it beat faster. Why not try running, dancing, skipping, swimming, or cycling? Keep going until you can feel your heart beating faster!

This chart shows a **heartbeat** before, during, and after exercise. When is the heart working hardest?

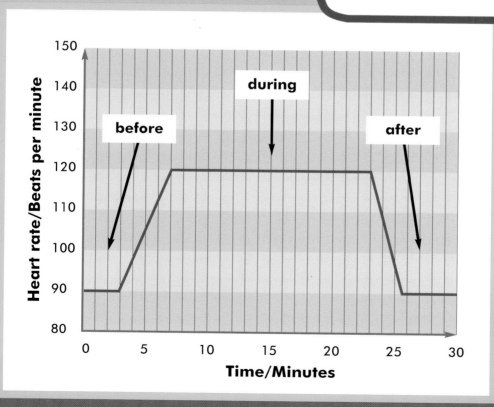

Which Foods Help You to Be Active?

Have you seen advertisements for sports drinks and energy bars? You don't need these things when you do exercise. A healthy, balanced diet will give your body all the energy it needs.

Eating for energy

You need to get active for a healthy body. But activity and exercise require fuel. **Carbohydrates** are foods that the body can easily use for energy. Healthy carbohydrates come from fruits, vegetables, and foods made from grains, such as bread, pasta, and rice.

If you want to be active, eat foods such as pasta and rice. They give you a lot of energy.

Eat well

You need to eat different kinds of foods. You should eat mostly fruits, vegetables, and grain foods. You should also eat some milk and dairy foods, and some beans, eggs, fish, and meat. You should eat only small amounts of foods and drinks that are high in fat or sugar.

Fruits and vegetables

Grain foods

Protein foods

Milk and dairy foods

Fatty and sugary foods

This food plate shows the proportions of foods you need.

Why You Need to Drink More Water

Your body is about two-thirds water. There is water in your blood, your skin, your **brain**—in fact all over your body. When you don't get enough water you will be **dehydrated**. You may feel tired, dizzy, and weak.

Sweating

When you are active you sweat more. Sweating is your body's way of cooling down. Water from inside the body comes through tiny holes onto the skin's surface. When this water dries in the air it takes some body heat with it, so you feel cooler. Drink before, during, and after exercise to replace the water lost as sweat.

You don't just get water from drinks. You can get water from juicy fruits such as watermelons.

Why not be active in water as well as drinking water when you're active?

Did you know?
You need to drink about eight glasses of water a day to keep your body hydrated.

13

Why Should You Wear a Helmet?

Why do you think helmets and pads are called safety gear? Because they keep you safe, of course! Rock climbers and hockey players wear helmets to protect their heads in case of a fall or bump. You should wear the right gear when you are active, too.

You should always wear kneepads for protection. A bad fall can break your bones and bruise or strain the muscles inside your body.

Use your head

A helmet protects the brain inside your **skull.** Your brain is the body's control center. Without it you cannot survive, so a helmet can save your life.

Get a grip

Sports gear is made for being active! Sneakers have treads that grip the ground so you can run and change direction quickly. Stretchy clothes, such as cycling shorts or bathing suits, allow you to move more easily.

Soccer shoes have studs to grip muddy fields.

Why Do Warm-ups Matter?

Have you ever had sore legs after playing sports? Or hurt yourself in a game? You should try doing warm-ups! Warm-ups are gentle exercises you do before being active. Doing five to ten minutes of warm-ups reduces the risk of soreness and injury.

How warm-ups work

Warm-ups increase the blood supply to your muscles. This makes the muscles warm and gives them more energy. That means they are able to move more easily.

Ways to warm up

- Brisk walking
- Skipping
- Slow jogging on the spot
- Stretching and bending
- Toe touches

Does your team do warm-ups before a match?

Cool down

You should always make sure that you cool down after exercise. This will help to prevent your legs from becoming sore or stiff later. Why not try stretching your muscles, walking, or jogging on the spot?

Runners usually jog for a few minutes after a race. This helps them cool down and allows their heart rates to get back to normal gently.

What Exercise is Best?

The best exercise is the one you like most.
If exercise isn't fun, it's hard to keep it up.
There are loads of activities that you can
try to see which you like best.

Give it a try

Why not try a new sport? Just think what fun
it would be to join a soccer or hockey team.
Maybe you would prefer an activity where
you stretch and bend, such as gymnastics or
dancing. Trying a new activity will boost
your confidence!

It doesn't matter
whether you like team
sports or just exercising
alone. The important
thing is to be active!

Mix it up

Try doing a mix of activities to exercise all the different parts of your body.

- Rowing and tennis are good for your arm muscles.
- Running and cycling are good for your leg muscles.
- Swimming works many muscles at once.

Don't miss out on the great feeling that you get when your team plays well. Get active and join in!

How Often Should You Exercise?

You should exercise for at least an hour every day. But you should be active during the rest of the day, too. Try to avoid spending too long in front of the TV or computer. You don't want to become a couch potato, do you?

If you find it hard to make time to be active, try walking to school.

Exercising every day helps you:

- Feel happy and look good
- Sleep soundly
- Build strong bones and muscles
- Stay at a healthy weight

What counts?

It is not just sports and exercise classes that count as being active. You can keep fit and healthy by helping around the house. Why not try washing the car or raking the leaves?

Now that you know why you need exercise to stay healthy, stop reading this book and get active!

Taking the dog for a walk will make you fit and your family will thank you for it, too!

Glossary

blood Red liquid found in tiny tubes, called blood vessels, inside the body. The blood carries food and oxygen around the body

bones The hard parts in the body that make up the skeleton

brain The part of the body found inside the skull. The brain controls the rest of the body

carbohydrates Types of food that provide energy. Rice and pasta are types of carbohydrates

dehydrated To be without enough water to work properly

energy Allows people to do everything they need to live, grow, and be active. Energy comes from the food we eat

heart A muscle that squeezes to pump blood around the body

heartbeat The beat of the heart muscle pumping again and again

limber Able to bend easily

muscles Parts of the body that allow you to move

oxygen A gas in the air. We breathe in air and the oxygen enters our blood deep inside our lungs

skeleton The framework of bones that gives your body its shape

skull The set of bones that forms your head and protects the brain

Further Information

Web sites

Sign up to be part of the President's Challenge and you could win awards for staying active:
http://fitness.gov/challenge/challenge.html

Learn more about health, fitness, and nutrition through fun articles, games, and recipes at:
http://www.kidnetic.com

Find out more about how to stay healthy at:
http://kidshealth.org/kid/

Books

How to Improve at... sports series.
Crabtree Publishing Company (2008-9)

Slim Goodbody's Body Buddies series by John Burstein.
Crabtree Publishing Company (2009)

Index

active lifestyle 20–21

blood 8, 12, 16
bones 6–7, 14, 20, 21
brain 12, 15

carbohydrates 10
clothes 15
cooling down 12, 17
cycling 9, 19

dehydrated 12

energy 4, 8, 10, 16
exercise 5, 9, 12, 14–19, 20

fat 11
flexible 6
food 8, 10–11
fruit 10, 11

gymnastics 6, 18

heart 8–9
heartbeat 9, 17
helmets 14–15

injury 7, 16

limber 6

muscles 6–7, 8, 14, 16,
   17, 19, 20, 21

overweight 4
oxygen 8

rest 5
running 9, 16, 19

skeleton 6
skull 15
sleep 5
soccer 15
sport 10, 12, 14–19
stretching 6, 17
strong 4, 6
sugar 11
sweat 12
swimming 13, 15, 19

team sports 19
trainers 15

vegetables 10, 11

warm-ups 16–17
water 12–13